PIANO ACCOMPANIMENT

MOVIE FAVORITES

Solos and Band Arrangements
Correlated with Essential Elements Band Method

Arranged by MICHAEL SWEENEY
Piano Accompaniments arranged by LLOYD CONLEY

Welcome to Essential Elements Movie Favorites! There are two versions of each selection in this versatile book. The SOLO version appears on the left-hand page of each student book. The FULL BAND arrangement appears on the right-hand page. The supplemental recording may be used as an accompaniment for solo performance. It may also be used as a teaching aid in full band rehearsals. Additional accompaniment recordings may be purchased separately in CD or cassette format.

Piano Accompaniment Page	Student Page	Title	Correlated with Essential Elements
2	3	Theme from "Jurassic Park"	Book 1, page 1
5	5	Chariots Of Fire	Book 1, page 19
8	7	The Man From Snowy River	Book 1, page 19
11	9	Forrest Gump – Main Title (Feather Theme)	Book 1, page 29
14	11	Somewhere Out There	Book 1, page 29
17	13	The John Dunbar Theme	Book 1, page 29
20	15	Raiders March	Book 2, page 14
23	17	Apollo 13 (End Credits)	Book 2, page 14
26	19	Theme From E.T. (The Extra-Terrestrial)	Book 2, page 14
29	21	Star Trek® - The Motion Picture	Book 2, page 29
33	23	Back To The Future	Book 2, page 29

ISBN 978-0-7935-5970-1

HAL•LEONARD® CORPORATION

7777 W. BLUEMOUND RD. P.O. BOX 13819 MILWAUKEE, WI 53213

Copyright © 1996 HAL LEONARD CORPORATION
International Copyright Secured   All Rights Reserved

00860026

From The Universal Motion Picture JURASSIC PARK

Theme From "JURASSIC PARK"

PIANO ACCOMPANIMENT

Composed by JOHN WILLIAMS
Arranged by MICHAEL SWEENEY

© Copyright 1993 by MUSIC CORPORATION OF AMERICA, INC.
This arrangement © Copyright 1996 by MUSIC CORPORATION OF AMERICA, INC.
International Copyright Secured   All Rights Reserved

MCA music publishing

00860026

CHARIOTS OF FIRE

PIANO ACCOMPANIMENT

Music by VANGELIS
Arranged by MICHAEL SWEENEY

© 1981 EMI MUSIC PUBLISHING LTD.
This arrangement © 1996 EMI MUSIC PUBLISHING LTD.
All Rights for the World, excluding Holland, Controlled and Administered by EMI APRIL MUSIC INC.
All Rights Reserved   International Copyright Secured   Used by Permission

From THE MAN FROM SNOWY RIVER

THE MAN FROM SNOWY RIVER
(Main Title Theme)

PIANO ACCOMPANIMENT

By BRUCE ROWLAND
Arranged by MICHAEL SWEENEY

© 1982 COLGEMS–EMI MUSIC INC. and BRUCE ROWLAND ENTERPRISES PTY. LTD.
This arrangement © 1996 COLGEMS–EMI MUSIC INC. and BRUCE ROWLAND ENTERPRISES PTY. LTD.
All Rights for the world excluding Australia, New Zealand and New Guinea Controlled and Administered by COLGEMS–EMI MUSIC INC.
All Rights Reserved   International Copyright Secured   Used by Permission

From The Paramount Motion Picture FORREST GUMP

FORREST GUMP - MAIN TITLE

(Feather Theme)

PIANO ACCOMPANIMENT

Music by ALAN SILVESTRI
Arranged by MICHAEL SWEENEY

Copyright © 1994 by Ensign Music Corporation
This arrangement Copyright © 1996 by Ensign Music Corporation
International Copyright Secured   All Rights Reserved

00860026

12

00860026

From AN AMERICAN TAIL

SOMEWHERE OUT THERE

PIANO ACCOMPANIMENT

Words and Music by JAMES HORNER,
BARRY MANN and CYNTHIA WEIL
Arranged by MICHAEL SWEENEY

© Copyright 1986 by MCA MUSIC PUBLISHING,
A Division of MCA INC. and MUSIC CORPORATION OF AMERICA, INC.
This arrangement © Copyright 1996 by MCA MUSIC PUBLISHING,
A Division of MCA INC. and MUSIC CORPORATION OF AMERICA, INC.
International Copyright Secured   All Rights Reserved

MCA music publishing

From **DANCES WITH WOLVES**
THE JOHN DUNBAR THEME

By JOHN BARRY
Arranged by MICHAEL SWEENEY

PIANO ACCOMPANIMENT

© 1990 EMI VIRGIN SONGS, INC., AFFIRMED MUSIC and TIG MUSIC
This arrangement © 1996 EMI VIRGIN SONGS, INC., AFFIRMED MUSIC and TIG MUSIC
All Rights for AFFIRMED MUSIC Controlled and Administered by EMI VIRGIN SONGS, INC.
All Rights for TIG MUSIC for the U.S. and Canada Administered by SONGS OF POLYGRAM INTERNATIONAL, INC.
All Rights Reserved   International Copyright Secured   Used by Permission

From The Paramount Motion Picture RAIDERS OF THE LOST ARK

RAIDERS MARCH

PIANO ACCOMPANIMENT

By JOHN WILLIAMS
Arranged by MICHAEL SWEENEY

Copyright © 1981 by Bantha Music and Ensign Music Corporation
This arrangement Copyright © 1996 by Bantha Music and Ensign Music Corporation
All Rights for the World Controlled and Administered by Ensign Music Corporation
International Copyright Secured   All Rights Reserved

00860026

From APOLLO 13
APOLLO 13
(End Credits)

PIANO ACCOMPANIMENT

By JAMES HORNER
Arranged by MICHAEL SWEENEY

© Copyright 1995 by MCA MUSIC PUBLISHING, A Division of MCA INC.
This arrangement © Copyright 1996 by MCA MUSIC PUBLISHING, A Division of MCA INC.
International Copyright Secured   All Rights Reserved

MCA music publishing

From The Universal Picture E.T. (THE EXTRA-TERRESTRIAL)

THEME FROM E.T. (THE EXTRA-TERRESTRIAL)

PIANO ACCOMPANIMENT

Music by JOHN WILLIAMS
Arranged by MICHAEL SWEENEY

© Copyright 1982 by MUSIC CORPORATION OF AMERICA, INC.
This arrangement © Copyright 1996 by MUSIC CORPORATION OF AMERICA, INC.
International Copyright Secured   All Rights Reserved

00860026

MCA music publishing

STAR TREK®-THE MOTION PICTURE

PIANO ACCOMPANIMENT

Music by JERRY GOLDSMITH
Arranged by MICHAEL SWEENEY

Copyright © 1979 by Ensign Music Corporation
This arrangement Copyright © 1996 by Ensign Music Corporation
International Copyright Secured   All Rights Reserved

00860026

From The Universal Motion Picture BACK TO THE FUTURE

BACK TO THE FUTURE

By ALAN SILVESTRI
Arranged by MICHAEL SWEENEY

PIANO ACCOMPANIMENT

© Copyright 1985 by MUSIC CORPORATION OF AMERICA, INC.
This arrangement © Copyright 1996 by MUSIC CORPORATION OF AMERICA, INC.
International Copyright Secured   All Rights Reserved

MCA music publishing

00860026